Advent Illustrated

Waiting 'Round the Wreath

A Seasons Illustrated

Bible Journaling

Study

by

Sara Laughed

For Bop, who has supported me in every season of my life.
Altijd jouw Kleine Beer.

TABLE OF CONTENTS

1

THE WONDER OF ADVENT

If you grew up celebrating Christmas, or even watching Christmas movies, you might be familiar with the famous poem by Clement Clarke Moore, "The Night Before Christmas." Though I never had this poem read to me as a child, I've heard the opening lines often enough to recite by heart:

> *'Twas the night before Christmas, when all through the house*
> *Not a creature was stirring, not even a mouse...*

Those two lines alone describe perfectly the magical

stillness of Christmas Eve. I remember lying in bed as a little girl, practically tingling with excitement, *waiting*: for sleep, for morning, for the wonder and delight of Christmas Day. The air seemed to hum with a kind of expectant energy, as though the world itself was holding its breath. An author might call this moment a *'pregnant pause.'*

Advent invites us into this pause, but for a moment that extends weeks prior to the night before Christmas. In the midst of the chaos of the holiday season and the humdrum routines our everyday lives, Advent asks us to make room for a quieter pace. In a world of instant gratification and *right-now* timing, Advent challenges us to give in to waiting; to sit in our expectancy. And in the depths of winter, as the days get shorter and the nights seem to cloak the world in darkness, Advent offers us a spark of hope; a taste of what is to come.

To me, this spark of hope is best displayed by the beauty of the Advent wreath. Each week, families and churches around the world gather around wreaths large and small to light candles. There are four candles placed around the wreath, one for every week of Advent. While the names and symbols of these weekly candles vary from denomination to denomination, when there is a fifth candle, is always the same: the white Christ candle in the center, to be lit on Christmas Day.

As we enter into the Advent season, I invite you to join me in preparing our spirits for the coming of the Christ child. Join me in these weeks of waiting as we journal through the themes of Hope, Peace, Love, and Joy, in anticipation of Christmas Day. Join me in this *'pregnant pause'* — a pause that holds not just excitement, but a holy expectancy, as it did for Mary all those years ago.

2

ABOUT ADVENT ILLUSTRATED

Advent Illustrated is a four-week Bible journaling challenge through the season of Advent. Bible journaling is a form of devotional art, in which people make art in the margins or pages of their Bibles, or in separate notebooks if they're so inclined. Often, this artwork is shared online in communities on Facebook, via blogs, or through other media. Seasons Illustrated, which writes and hosts Advent Illustrated, has its own Facebook community, called Seasons Illustrated Bible Journaling. Please join us!

The Seasons Illustrated Bible Journaling community differs from other Bible journaling groups in two ways. The first is that it offers Bible studies with a creative twist, which dig into the Biblical text and offer context and optional prompts to guide you in your journaling. We hope that the additional knowledge and interpretation will help you to develop a more meaningful journaling practice.

The second point of difference is that several of our studies center around the liturgical seasons. Advent is the first season of the 'liturgical year,' or Christian calendar, which walks us through the year with an eye on the story of Jesus. These seasons, which include Advent, Christmas, Epiphany, Lent, Eastertide, Pentecost, and Ordinary Time, are explained at further length in Chapter 3.

While Advent is a time of waiting, our culture doesn't bend to that easily. We may wish to have a slow and thoughtful Advent, but thanks to the rush of the holiday season and the pressures of everyday life, that may not always be within reach. For that reason, the Advent Illustrated challenge is designed to be customizable. There are six different plans, ranging from daily journaling to a once-per-week practice. Further, the daily readings are meant to be short reflections that should only take a few minutes to read, meaning that you can reflect on them at home in your devotional corner, while waiting in the pick-up line at your child's school, or during your 15-minute break at work.

Finally, while this is a Bible journaling 'challenge,' please remember that nothing is required of you! We hope to add some additional meaning and structure to your Advent season, but not at the cost of your peace of mind. If you need to skip a day to rest, take care of someone you love, or read one more bedtime story, then go ahead. Better to illustrate the love of Advent in the moments of our lives than in the pages of our Bibles.

That said, I am so excited to have you joining us for Advent this year. I can't wait to journal and worship alongside you. But before we get started, let's take a closer look at Advent and the liturgical year.

3

INTRODUCTION TO THE LITURGICAL YEAR

The liturgical year, also called the Christian year or church year, is the cycle of seasons and celebrations that make up the Christian calendar. Some of these are well-known across denominations: the holy days of Christmas and Easter, for example, or the season of Lent. Others, like the season of Ordinary Time, are lesser-known, but beautiful and meaningful in their own right. This chapter serves as a basic introduction to the liturgical seasons for those of you for whom it is new or unfamiliar.

The liturgical year is made up of a series of seasons that each have distinct themes, colors, and even means of practice or prayer. You may attend a church where the paraments, or hangings on the altar, change color throughout the year; these colors reflect the liturgical colors of each season. The liturgical seasons walk us through the year with a focus on the life and ministry of Jesus.

Advent is the beginning of the liturgical year, so the first Sunday of Advent is a Christian "New Year's" of sorts. The season of Advent focuses on the themes of anticipation, preparation, and the coming of Christ. The liturgical color of Advent is purple, although the third week of Advent uses the color pink to symbolize love or mercy.

Advent is followed by the liturgical season of Christmas, which lasts twelve days; this is where the "Twelve Days of Christmas" comes from! The Christmas season focuses on the themes of peace, fulfillment, and celebration. The liturgical colors of Christmas are white and gold.

Christmas is followed by Epiphany, lasting until Ash Wednesday. Some traditions celebrate the feast of Epiphany and then Ordinary Time, while others celebrate Epiphany as its own season. Epiphany's colors are white and gold. This season focuses on the themes of God making God's work known through the life and ministry of Christ.

Following Epiphany is the season of Lent, focusing on reflection, repentance, and renewal. The liturgical color of Lent is purple. Lent begins with Ash Wednesday and continues through Holy Week until Easter.

The season of Easter celebrates the themes of resurrection and life. Its liturgical colors are white and gold. It is followed by the longest season, that of Ordinary Time, focusing on the rhythms and rituals of daily life. Ordinary

Time is represented by the color green, and lasts until the year begins again with Advent.

These seasons, and the holy days and feast days that punctuate them, walk us through the year with an eye to the life, ministry, and legacy of Christ. The seasons are a blessing because, like the non-religious holidays that bring us joy through family, tradition, and values, they help us celebrate what matters most to us. Not just family, but a worldwide community of believers of all backgrounds. Not just tradition, but a legacy of thousands of years of faith and knowledge, passed down to us. Not just values, but a deep and resounding belief that amplifies our celebration and recognizes us in our deepest and most difficult places.

This calendar of seasons and holy days meets us where we are and reminds us why we're here. If you have spent your life living with the liturgical year, I hope that this study can invite you to spend more time in your own practice and perhaps dig deeper into this season. If the liturgical seasons are new to you, then I hope that this Advent study will help ignite in you the same passion that I feel for the liturgical year. May it be a blessing to you!

4

HOW TO START BIBLE JOURNALING

Advent Illustrated is unique to other Advent studies because it engages in the devotional practice of Bible journaling. Many people participating are excited to begin Bible journaling, but don't know where to start. I know that taking notes in your Bible can be a little intimidating, let alone drawing, lettering, and painting in it! For that reason, this chapter will be a brief guide on how to get started in your journaling Bible for those of you who haven't yet.

Understanding what it's all about

Bible journaling is not about making the most beautiful art. I, myself, am guilty of wanting to make something really beautiful and impressive for the sake of, well… making something really beautiful and impressive! But that attitude isn't as fulfilling and meaningful as one that dwells in practice. Journaling isn't about the outcome, it's about the process. Focus on connecting with what you're doing, and the skill will come with time.

Finding a verse

You have your Bible, your pen(s), and maybe some extras, like paints, stamps, or stickers. (If you don't yet, check out some recommendations in the next chapter!) The next thing to do is find a verse.

Bible journaling can be a little scary, especially if you're not used to writing in your Bible. I recommend starting off with a verse that you know well and that means a lot to you. Beginning with a verse that you are familiar with helps take away some level of discomfort when it comes to journaling in your Bible for the first time, and it may spark an idea faster. But choose a verse you know and like before journaling your favorite verse. If you choose your absolute favorite, it may be difficult to come up with a design that includes everything it means to you. Start small until you're comfortable.

Getting inspired

I'm a creative soul, but I'm not an artistic soul. I find it difficult to come up with entirely new designs for things.

I like to find inspiration – and with the internet, that's easier to do now than ever.

You can use Pinterest to browse designs that inspire you, or you can join a Bible journaling group on Facebook, such as our group, Seasons Illustrated Bible Journaling. You can also do a Google search for "Bible journaling" and the verse you chose, to see designs that other people have done with that same verse! Finding inspiration in places like these is a great way to get started with Bible journaling and figure out your style and the kinds of art you'd like to try.

Getting started

Now comes the exciting part! Once you have your tools and verse, it's time to get started. Everyone has a different process for how they do this; for me, it helps to begin in prayer. In the end, what it comes down to is mustering up the courage to put pen to paper and make something that expresses how you feel.

This is my method for the actual journaling process:

1. *Reflect on the verse.* Read it over a few times; maybe do a little background reading. Let it sink into your bones. I think about the parts of the verse that mean something to me, and then I try to figure out how I can represent them in art.

2. *Sketch it out with a pencil.* I like to use a simple mechanical pencil to do my sketching so that I don't make any permanent mistakes!

3. *Outline it with pen.* I use my skinny Pigma Microns to do this, as they don't bleed through the paper. You can read about them in the next chapter.

4. *Fill it in with color.* Next, I use gel pens, colored pencils, and watercolor pencils to add color and dimension to my design.

That's it! Everyone's process is different, but starting with a small and simple design may be helpful if you haven't journaled before. Once you get more comfortable with Bible journaling, you can go ahead and experiment with paints, stamps, and stickers. The Word is your canvas!

4

BASIC SUPPLIES FOR BIBLE JOURNALING

I'll start by saying that you need absolutely nothing to do Bible journaling other than a Bible and a pen. Really. You may have seen people with beautiful paints, stamps, and tabs in their Bibles, but all of those people got started with what you probably already have in your house.

That said, if you'd like to buy a special journaling Bible or you would like to invest in pens that don't bleed through thin paper, I have some recommendations.

Favorite Bible: Black ESV Single Column Journaling Bible by Crossway

Crossway has a very beautiful selection of Bibles that are specifically intended for Bible journaling. The two that I use, shown in the photos throughout this book, are two editions of the ESV single column journaling Bible. I love that this Bible opens flat, whether you're flipping open to Genesis or Revelation. I also really love the cream-colored paper and the size and font of the text.

Favorite pens: Sakura Pigma Micron 01 Ink Pen Set

Having used gel pens, rollerballs, and a variety of other pens on Bible paper, I can say that bleed-through is a huge problem. It's frustrating and it makes the other side of the paper harder to read. Pigma Micron pens are designed for archival paper, so the ink does not bleed through, even on very thin paper like that found in most Bibles. The tips are very fine, so it is easy to take small notes in the margins, or make bigger doodles.

Favorite highlighters: Zebra Eco Zebrite Double-Ended Highlighters

When it comes to liquid highlighters, these are my favorite for Bible journaling by far. They go on smoothly and don't bleed through the paper. I use the fine-tip highlighters so I can highlight line by line if I want to. As with the Pigma Micron pens, these highlighters "ghost" through the paper a little, meaning you can see a touch of color on the other side — but there is no bleed through, and the ghosting is less than I have had with any other product.

Other products

In addition to these products, I use colored pencils, watercolor pencils, washi tape, and other products. Many other people use stamps and stickers — it's all up to you! Go through your house or your local craft store and find the things that inspire you. Good luck and have fun!

5

SCHEDULE AND PLANS

In the weeks leading up to Christmas, we are often swept up in a series of to do's. Buy turkey. Vacuum the pine needles under the tree. Finish the gift for him, find the perfect one for her, wrap the cookbook you found for so-and-so. When our Christmas seasons are grounded in the Christian tradition, the time we spend in prayer, church, or worship should feel like a welcome respite from that stress; but sometimes, even *that* feels like just another 'to do.'

I hope that Advent Illustrated will be a time of connection and devotion for you, rather than yet another thing to add to your daily checklist. For that reason, the Advent Illustrated program is customizable to your schedule and needs. This year, there are six plans, ranging from once weekly to six times per week.

The program

This year's Advent Illustrated challenge centers around the themes of the Advent wreath: Hope, Peace, Love, and Joy. Each week will feature a selection of verses centered around that week's theme. Each week features four different kinds of days:

1. **Rest days** are our day of preparation and reflection. For those participating in the six-day Wreath plan, these will fall on Sundays.
2. On **Scripture** days, we journal verses from the Old and New Testaments.
3. On **Story** days, we will explore the Nativity story and celebrate the coming of the Christ child.
4. On **Song** days, we will enjoy one of the four traditional songs from the Old Testament and the Nativity narrative.

Each day, excluding Rest Days, comes with a verse that our community will be journaling together. The daily readings will include the verse, some context, and a creative prompt for that day to get your artistic juices flowing. Whether you journal once a week, twice a week, or six days a week, I recommend that you do the daily readings so you can follow the entire arc of the Nativity story and readings.

This chapter includes the six plans that you can choose to follow this Advent season. Each plan is named after a different component of the Advent wreath!

- **Wreath** (6 days a week) Using this plan, you will participate in every day of our challenge, exploring four verses relating to the weekly theme, and experiencing both the story and songs of the Nativity. The Scripture days will feature an Old Testament verse, a Psalm verse, a Gospel verse, and an Epistle verse from Paul's letters.

- **Cedar** (5 days a week). This plan includes three Scripture days and both the Story and Song days. The Scripture days will include an Old Testament verse, a Psalm selection, and a selection from Paul's epistles.

- **Laurel** (4 day a week). In this plan, journalers will enjoy a Song day, a Story day, and two Scripture days. The Scripture days will include a Gospel and Epistle selection every week.

- **Holly** (3 days a week). This plan includes a weekly Story day, and two Scripture days every week, including one Old Testament verse and one Gospel verse.

- **Ivy** (2 days a week). This plan includes only the Story and Song days, and no Scripture days.

- **Rosemary** (1 day a week). This one-per-week plan includes the Nativity story spread out over four weeks, and does not include Song or Scripture days.

The following pages include a paginated verse chart for each of the Advent plans.

WREATH – 6 DAYS A WEEK

WEEK	DAY	READING	PG.
Hope	Rest	*First week of Advent*	35
	Scripture – OT	Isaiah 9:2	37
	Scripture – Psalm	Psalm 62:5	39
	Story	Isaiah 9:6	41
	Song	Psalm 130	43
	Scripture – Gospel	John 8:12	45
	Scripture – Epistle	Romans 15:13	47
Peace	Rest	*Second week of Advent*	49
	Scripture – OT	Isaiah 54:10	50
	Scripture – Psalm	Psalm 29:11	52
	Story	Luke 1:30-33	54
	Song	Luke 1:46-50	56
	Scripture – Gospel	John 16:33	58
	Scripture – Epistle	2 Thess. 3:16	60
Love	Rest	*Third week of Advent*	62
	Scripture – OT	Leviticus 19:18	63
	Scripture – Psalm	Psalm 59:16	65
	Story	Matthew 1:18-25	67
	Song	Luke 1:68-79	69
	Scripture – Gospel	John 13:34-35	72
	Scripture – Epistle	1 Cor. 13:4-8	74
Joy	Rest	*Fourth week of Advent*	76
	Scripture – OT	Nehemiah 8:10	78
	Scripture – Psalm	Psalm 30:5	80
	Story	Luke 2:1, 2:4-14	82
	Song	Luke 2:29-32	84
	Scripture – Gospel	Matthew 2:9-11	86
	Scripture – Epistle	1 Peter 1:8-9	88

CEDAR – 5 DAYS A WEEK

WEEK	DAY	READING	PG.
Hope	Rest	*First week of Advent*	35
	Scripture – OT	Isaiah 9:2	37
	Scripture – Psalm	Psalm 62:5	39
	Story	Isaiah 9:6	41
	Song	Psalm 130	43
	Scripture – Epistle	Romans 15:13	47
Peace	Rest	*Second week of Advent*	49
	Scripture – OT	Isaiah 54:10	50
	Scripture – Psalm	Psalm 29:11	52
	Story	Luke 1:30-33	54
	Song	Luke 1:46-50	56
	Scripture – Epistle	2 Thess. 3:16	60
Love	Rest	*Third week of Advent*	62
	Scripture – OT	Leviticus 19:18	63
	Scripture – Psalm	Psalm 59:16	65
	Story	Matthew 1:18-25	67
	Song	Luke 1:68-79	69
	Scripture – Epistle	1 Cor. 13:4-8	74
Joy	Rest	*Fourth week of Advent*	76
	Scripture – OT	Nehemiah 8:10	78
	Scripture – Psalm	Psalm 30:5	80
	Story	Luke 2:1, 2:4-14	82
	Song	Luke 2:29-32	84
	Scripture – Epistle	1 Peter 1:8-9	88

LAUREL – 4 DAYS A WEEK

WEEK	DAY	READING	PG.
Hope	Rest	*First week of Advent*	35
	Story	Isaiah 9:6	41
	Song	Psalm 130	43
	Scripture – Gospel	John 8:12	45
	Scripture – Epistle	Romans 15:13	47
Peace	Rest	*Second week of Advent*	49
	Story	Luke 1:30-33	54
	Song	Luke 1:46-50	56
	Scripture – Gospel	John 16:33	58
	Scripture – Epistle	2 Thess. 3:16	60
Love	Rest	*Third week of Advent*	62
	Story	Matthew 1:18-25	67
	Song	Luke 1:68-79	69
	Scripture – Gospel	John 13:34-35	72
	Scripture – Epistle	1 Cor. 13:4-8	74
Joy	Rest	*Fourth week of Advent*	76
	Story	Luke 2:1, 2:4-14	82
	Song	Luke 2:29-32	84
	Scripture – Gospel	Matthew 2:9-11	86
	Scripture – Epistle	1 Peter 1:8-9	88

HOLLY – 3 DAYS A WEEK

WEEK	DAY	READING	PG.
Hope	Rest	*First week of Advent*	35
	Scripture – OT	Isaiah 9:2	37
	Story	Isaiah 9:6	41
	Scripture – Gospel	John 8:12	45
Peace	Rest	*Second week of Advent*	49
	Scripture – OT	Isaiah 54:10	50
	Story	Luke 1:30-33	54
	Scripture – Gospel	John 16:33	58
Love	Rest	*Third week of Advent*	62
	Scripture – OT	Leviticus 19:18	63
	Story	Matthew 1:18-25	67
	Scripture – Gospel	John 13:34-35	72
Joy	Rest	*Fourth week of Advent*	76
	Scripture – OT	Nehemiah 8:10	78
	Story	Luke 2:1, 2:4-14	82
	Scripture – Gospel	Matthew 2:9-11	86

IVY – 2 DAYS A WEEK

WEEK	DAY	READING	PG.
Hope	Rest	*First week of Advent*	35
	Story	Isaiah 9:6	41
	Song	Psalm 130	43
Peace	Rest	*Second week of Advent*	49
	Story	Luke 1:30-33	54
	Song	Luke 1:46-50	56
Love	Rest	*Third week of Advent*	62
	Story	Matthew 1:18-25	67
	Song	Luke 1:68-79	69
Joy	Rest	*Fourth week of Advent*	76
	Story	Luke 2:1, 2:4-14	82
	Song	Luke 2:29-32	84

ROSEMARY – 1 DAY A WEEK

WEEK	DAY	READING	PG.
Hope	Rest	*First week of Advent*	35
	Story	Isaiah 9:6	41
Peace	Rest	*Second week of Advent*	49
	Story	Luke 1:30-33	54
Love	Rest	*Third week of Advent*	62
	Story	Matthew 1:18-25	67
Joy	Rest	*Fourth week of Advent*	76
	Story	Luke 2:1, 2:4-14	82

7

ADVENT SELECTIONS

Now that you've gotten familiar with Advent Illustrated and our plans for this year, it's time to dig into your Bible. I recommend that, no matter what plan you're on, you read the daily context and prompt to help you follow along.

Just like the Advent wreath has four themed candles to mark the four weeks leading up to Christmas, this study has four weekly themes: Hope, Peace, Love, and Joy. We begin each week by noting the absence of our weekly theme, or reflecting on the things that make it more difficult to fully experience that quality. Then, throughout the week as we look at verses from the Old Testament and the Psalms; the nativity story and the canticles (hymns) that it holds; and the Gospels and Epistles in the New Testament, we journey from hopelessness to hope, from violence to peace, from anger to love, and from sorrow to joy. With each passing day and week, we move closer to Christmas and prepare our hearts and minds for the coming of the Christ child on Christmas Day. I hope you are as excited as I am to get started. Let's begin!

REST DAY

–

FIRST WEEK OF ADVENT

Today is the first Sunday of Advent. For some of us, it is a welcome change; today marks the beginning of a new season, a new start, and a new year in the Christian calendar. But for others, the time leading up to Christmas is not a joy, but a stressor. Especially for many parents and grandparents, the holidays are a time when we are tasked with managing the world around us; between church events, school projects, gift-shopping, and keeping the house in one piece, devotional time can feel like yet another item on our daily list of tasks, instead of a welcome break from the rush of the outside world.

For that reason, we begin this week of Advent with a day of rest. Every Sunday, instead of a journaling prompt, we will come together to experience a moment of peace in the midst of this busy and exciting season. If you are eager to jump right in, today is the perfect day to prep your pages for Bible journaling, or to explore this guide and become familiar with the verses that we will be journaling this week. If, on the other hand, you need a moment to take a deep breath before getting started, then this is your invitation.

In this first week of Advent, we light the first purple candle in our wreath, symbolizing Hope. As members of the Seasons Illustrated community, this week we are also journaling and experiencing the hope of the Advent season. Each week in this study seeks to be a journey in itself, from a place of difficulty to a place of hope, peace, love, and joy. As we walk through our scriptural selections and the opening verses of the Nativity story, we will focus on the theme of hopefulness in the dark, and the hope embodied in the life and story Jesus. I am so happy to have you joining us this week - welcome to Advent!

—

ISAIAH 9:2

Verse:

The people who walked in darkness
have seen a great light;
those who dwelt in a land of deep darkness,
on them has light shone.

Isaiah 9:2

Context and prompt:

Advent is the story of a new beginning. At the time of Jesus' birth, God's people are living under occupation by the Romans. They live in darkness, waiting for freedom from political oppression, and for spiritual liberation through the coming of the Messiah. In the midst of that difficult wait, a child is born to a virgin in Bethlehem: Jesus, who is Immanuel, God with Us.

We so often rush to make it to that part of the story. But this week, we focus instead on hope in the waiting. Today's verse is taken from the Old Testament book of Isaiah; the darkness to which the author refers is the hiding of the Lord's face during the rule of a corrupt king. But, in part because it is quoted in the book of Matthew (Matthew 4:15), and in part because it seems to fit so well our understandings of the setting of the Christmas story, this verse is often related to the ministry of Jesus.

God's people walked in darkness, living in a time when God and God's presence did not feel tangible and present. Not only that, but they lived in a land of that darkness; it encompassed and surrounded them. In that difficult time, they saw the light; in the Gospels, that light is embodied in the life and love of Jesus. As we are reminded by John 1:5, "The light shines in the darkness, and the darkness has not overcome it."

As you journal the Isaiah verse today, consider the image of the light shining in the darkness. You might choose to illustrate fireflies in a mason jar, or a bonfire on a cold night, or even the first candle in the Advent wreath on a cold and cozy night. You could also letter the word "light," or write out the verse in warm yellows and oranges. Remember that there is no wrong way to do this; just pick up your pen and get started!

—

PSALM 62:5

Verse:

For God alone, O my soul, wait in silence,
for my hope is from him.

Psalm 62:5

Context and prompt:

Advent comes to us in winter. As the nights grow longer and the cold fog of December sets in, many of us retreat into our homes and our own selves. We struggle with the darkness and gloom of the winter season, in which the bare branches of the trees scratch at the sky, and blankets of snow seem to cloak the world in silence. In that time, the excitement of Christmas - twinkle lights, holiday music, and seasonal celebrations - brings us excitement for things to come. This is Advent: the season of waiting, of not-yet, of things to come.

In the same way that moments of excitement and anticipation light up the winter nights, the hope of the Christmas story tells us of what is to come. We sit in expectant hope, waiting for Christ to come, waiting for the fulfillment of our promises and stories. We make peace with the discomfort of waiting, and we find hope in our

God.

As you journal today's verse, focus on the feeling of waiting. For you, does waiting feel like a child itching to open her Christmas presents? Or is it a moment of sitting alone in the darkness, praying for good news? How you choose to illustrate this faithful and expectant wait is up to you; but whether you illustrate it with the examples above, or simply letter the words of this verse, remember that God provides a hope, even in the darkness.

ISAIAH 9:6

Verse:

For to us a child is born,
to us a son is given;
and the government shall be upon his shoulder,
and his name shall be called
Wonderful Counselor, Mighty God,
Everlasting Father, Prince of Peace.

Isaiah 9:6

Context and prompt:

Long before the Christ child, long before the Nativity, long before the visitation of the angel Gabriel to Mary, was a hope. Generations before Jesus came to the world, there were already people praying, waiting, and hoping for the fulfilment of the promise, and the coming of the Prince of Peace. Today is a Story day, in which we journal the story of the Nativity, and so some might expect us to begin with the moment that a young girl living in Galilee learns that she will bear the son of God. But the story of the Nativity doesn't begin with Mary. It begins with a hopeful and expectant wait.

This verse falls in the first portion of the Book of Isaiah, which focuses on the restoration of Judah and Jerusalem; but for Christians, it is a prophecy about the birth of Jesus. Though the verses are in the past-tense, they actually refer to what is to come; they are written in the past-tense to indicate the author's certainty that this child will be born, that the son will be given, and that he will be the Prince of Peace.

While we sometimes wait in fear, or angst, or with a wish that we think may not be fulfilled, Christians today can hope with the same certainty of Isaiah. The child was born, the son was given, and he is the Wonderful Counselor, Mighty God, Everlasting Father, Prince of Peace. Our expectant wait this Advent is one of both hope and celebration.

As you journal this verse today, reflect on the certainty and celebration that comes with waiting in Advent. What are your hopes for this season, and for Christmas? What burdens are you carrying that you hope may be eased? For today's page, you may wish to show someone in darkness, envisioning the birth of Jesus, or a child falling asleep and imagining Christmas Day. You could also letter the words of the verse "For to us a child is born," or simply illustrate the baby Jesus lying in the manger. Whatever you choose to journal today, let the spirit of hopeful certainty guide you!

PSALM 130:5-8 – DE PROFUNDIS

Verse:

I wait for the Lord, my soul waits,
and in his word I hope;
my soul waits for the Lord
more than watchmen for the morning,
more than watchmen for the morning.
O Israel, hope in the Lord!
For with the Lord there is steadfast love,
and with him is plentiful redemption.
And he will redeem Israel
from all his iniquities.

Psalm 130:5-8

Context and prompt:

Psalm 130, often referred to as De Profundis when set to music, is a song of hope and anticipation. Unlike our other three Song selections, it is not sung by a figure in the Nativity story; but it is an example of the expectant and hopeful waiting that we are focusing on this week. You can find this psalm set to music by searching for "De Profundis" on YouTube or by listening to the Advent Illustrated 2017 playlist.

When we wait in Advent, we are not just waiting for

the Christ child to be born. We are also waiting God's kingdom; for it to be on earth as it is in heaven. In the difficult times in which we live, it is easy to feel discouraged or overwhelmed by all the work that remains to be done. But we are called to be agents of Jesus' goodness in the world, just as we are called to remember that God is the restorer and redeemer of all things. This psalm calls us to wait for the Lord, and remember his steadfast love and redemption.

As you journal this verse today, I encourage you to focus on this theme of love and redemption. What does it mean to you? You may wish to draw a heart, or the arms of God sweeping you up. You may also wish to combine the imagery of the Nativity and the Easter story, to highlight the 'reason for the season.' You could even choose to letter the words "the reason for the season" over this psalm and its focus on love and redemption. Whichever direction you take this verse in, let yourself be guided by a spirit of devotion and not of self-consciousness. This is a devotional practice: let yourself get swept up in worship!

—

JOHN 8:12

Verse:

Again Jesus spoke to them, saying, "I am the light of the world. Whoever follows me will not walk in darkness, but will have the light of life."

John 8:12

Context and prompt:

Throughout this week, we have focused on waiting in hope despite darkness. Some verses from our study have focused on waiting for the light; others have emphasized making peace with our own discomfort in the dark. Today's verse offers a concrete hope for us: a promise that, when we follow Jesus, we have "the light of life." This is a spiritual inner Light distinct from the physical light that we experience as a part of creation. It is a Light that can guide and comfort us through times of difficulty. This is what Jesus offers, and it is the coming and celebration of this light that we wait for throughout Advent.

In journaling this verse, I encourage you to focus on what it means to have the light of life rather than walking in the darkness. You might wish to draw yourself walking beside Jesus, or illustrate what "the light of life" means to you. Is it love? Redemption? Peace? You could also choose to letter the phrase "the light of life" over the page. Let your hope for this feeling of Light guide you as you journal today.

ROMANS 15:13

Verse:

May the God of hope fill you with all joy and peace in believing, so that by the power of the Holy Spirit you may abound in hope.

Romans 15:13

Context and prompt:

We end the first week of Advent, focusing on Hope, with this verse from Paul in his letter to the Romans. These words come at the end of a section of the letter focusing on Christ as hope for both Jewish people and Gentiles. In the history of the early church, there was some debate about whether followers of Jesus could come from non-Jewish backgrounds, and here Paul is affirming that Jesus is hope for all, regardless of background or ethnicity. After several verses on this, Paul closes the section with this wish for joy and peace in believing, so that God's people may abound in hope.

Belief is not an easy journey, and almost all of us struggle with confusion, frustration, or doubt in at one time or another. A life of faith comes with its own seasons; just as the seasons of the year, these can be full of rich vibrancy and growth, or be as stark and sterile as winter. For those of us in the Northern Hemisphere, Advent falls during winter; but even when the trees are bare and the birds have flown south, there is still life, hiding and waiting for a warmer season. It will bud and blossom again; there is hope. Wherever you are in your spiritual life, whether in a summer or winter season, know that there is hope.

This is the final verse in our week on Hope. As you journal it today, focus on what you are hopeful for. What is bringing you comfort and excitement this season? What brings you joy? What are you looking forward to, or hoping will come to you, either again or for the first time? You may wish to journal reflections on any of these questions, or to focus on the word "Hope" on your page.

REST DAY
—
SECOND WEEK OF ADVENT

Welcome to the second week of Advent. This is a time of rest for everyone journaling with us this Advent, whether on the one-day or six-day plan. For those of you who are eager to journal or who have taken pauses throughout the week, today is a great time to catch up on pages you missed last week or prepare for the week to come. For those of us who are looking for some space in which to find a moment of peace in the midst of a busy season, let this day be that space for you.

Over the course of the last week, we journaled through the theme of Hope, beginning in a place darkness, and ending on a note of our hopes for the Advent season. For our second week, we light the candle of Peace, the second purple candle in our wreath. Throughout this week, we will focus on both outer and inner peace; facing and addressing the challenges of the world in which we live, but also creating peaceful hearts within ourselves.

Advent is a time of in-betweens: a time to wait for the things that are not-yet, and a time to celebrate what we have and what is to come. As we juggle this peculiar balance throughout this season, I pray that you see this week as both a time to celebrate the peaceful places in your life, and a call to recognize the places that are yearning for relief. As we wait for the birth of the Prince of Peace, may we be moved to use our hearts and hands to bring to this world what peace we can.

–

ISAIAH 54:10

Verse:

"For the mountains may depart
and the hills be removed,
but my steadfast love shall not depart from you,
and my covenant of peace shall not be removed,"
says the Lord, who has compassion on you.

Isaiah 54:10

Context and prompt:

The second week of Advent focuses on the theme of peace. It may seem almost foolish to wish for a peaceful world in a time where our own world can seem so swept up in violence. But then we remember the world into which Jesus was born: this world, our world, in a time just as trying and difficult as ours. Into this world a baby was born who would become the King of Kings, the Prince of Peace.

For many people, this has been a trying year. Across the world and within our own homes are places crying out for peace. As Christians, we struggle to acknowledge this difficulty while at the same time knowing that God is here, and that the love of God is with us even in the most difficult and trying of times. Our verse today reminds us to have faith: that no matter how tumultuous we find this time, whether the very mountains and hills are wiped away,

God's steadfast love is here, and the covenant of peace will always be with us.

–

PSALM 29:11

Verse:

May the Lord give strength to his people!
May the Lord bless his people with peace!

Psalm 29:11

Context and prompt:

It is said that we should turn to God both in times of prosperity and in times of hardship. As many of us know, that is easier said than done. When times are challenging, we have a hard time turning to God in the face of our own struggles and grief; and when our cup feels like it's overflowing, it can be challenging to make time for God. But through both the times when we push God aside, and through the times where we truly devote ourselves to our faith and practices, God is still there, loving and watching over us.

The verse above, excerpted from the Psalms, asks God to not only be there for us, but to provide strength and peace. When we are stuck in the depths of our own struggles, it can be challenging to believe or even ask for God to provide for us. But we find, through our faith, both strength and peace even in hard times. Strength by leaning on our faith, or our family, or by tuning into the deepest parts of ourselves. Peace by making the time to rest, to think, to pray.

Strength and peace can look more similar than you might have imagined. Sometimes, choosing to create peace in our lives and in the lives of others is the stronger, braver choice - especially in a world as challenged and war-torn as the one in which we live.

As you journal today, focus on the idea of strength and peace. When those two qualities are brought together, what does it look like to you? It could be a friend who is persisting gracefully despite tough times. It might be someone doing some small part to bring peace into their lives, in the face of challenges. Or it could be Jesus, who paid the ultimate price so that we would have peace and everlasting life. What strength that took. Journal any of these figures or whatever comes into your head today.

LUKE 1:30-33

Verse:

"And the angel said to her, "Do not be afraid, Mary, for you have found favor with God. And behold, you will conceive in your womb and bear a son, and you shall call his name Jesus. He will be great and will be called the Son of the Most High. And the Lord God will give to him the throne of his father David, and he will reign over the house of Jacob forever, and of his kingdom there will be no end."

Luke 1:30-33

Context and prompt:

When picturing the Son of God coming to earth - God putting on skin and sandals to experience life alongside us - it is easy to imagine the glory and splendor that is fit for a king. But when God came to earth, it was not in the form of a ruler or a wealthy merchant or someone with high status. Instead, God came to a young single mother in a small town in the middle of nowhere. How beautiful that God lived among those who were just like us.

Mary was just a young girl, most likely in her early teen years, when God chose her to carry the Son of God. In the passage above, the angel Gabriel appears to Mary to tell her for the first time that she will become pregnant. Gabriel tells her not to be afraid - a phrase that is often repeated when angels appear to humans in the New Testament. We don't hear Mary's response, but she must have felt something - a tremor, a quake in her heart, or maybe excitement at the words of the angel. When Gabriel says that she would call the baby's name Jesus, and that he would receive the throne of David and reign over the house of Jacob, Mary must have felt fear or joy or pleasure; not only because she would carry the Son of God, but also because the Son of God would appear to the world, fulfilling the promises that had been made so long ago. To his Kingdom there would be no end - it would last longer than Mary and than the world itself. Longer than anything she could have ever imagined for herself and the future of her children.

Today, we focus on Mary and on Gabriel as we journal this verse. Imagine the angel Gabriel appearing to Mary; consider sketching the two of them together, as Gabriel tells Mary of what will happen. Or you may want to illustrate Mary herself experiencing the joy and fear and confusion that she must have experienced at Gabriel's news. Finally, you could choose to letter a phrase from this verse that you find meaningful or memorable - perhaps "Son of the Most High" or "there will be no end." Whatever you choose to journal, let the spirit of wonder overtake you as you create in the margins of your Bible today.

SONG
—
LUKE 1:46-50 –
MAGNIFICAT

Verse:

And Mary said,
"My soul magnifies the Lord,
and my spirit rejoices in God my Savior,
for he has looked on the humble estate of his servant.
For behold, from now on all generations will call me blessed;
for he who is mighty has done great things for me,
and holy is his name.
And his mercy is for those who fear him
from generation to generation."

Luke 1:46-50

Context and prompt:

After Mary becomes pregnant, she travels to visit her cousin, Elizabeth. Elizabeth is elderly, and has also recently become pregnant due to God's action and intervention in the world - in fact, her husband Zechariah was also visited by the angel Gabriel to tell him that Elizabeth would conceive a son.

Mary and Elizabeth must have had a special bond - not only because they were cousins, but because they were pregnant at the same time. They may not know yet how the lives of their children will play out, but Elizabeth's son

John will become known as John the Baptist; he will prepare the way for Jesus and eventually baptize him. When Mary and Elizabeth see each other for the first time when they are both pregnant, John leaps in his mother's womb, and she cries out a blessing to Mary, and Mary responds with words that have been immortalized in song as the Magnificat. These words are still today played in song because they indicate not only Mary's joy at her own pregnancy, but also her trust in the fulfillment of God's promises.

As you journal today, focus on the image of Mary's song. Maybe you would like to illustrate Mary singing joyfully, mouth open. Maybe you would prefer to play with the imagery of the music, illustrating music lines over the page or in the margins of your Bible. Or perhaps you would like to letter the words of Mary's opening line, "My soul does magnify the Lord." Let Mary's wonder and peaceful trust guide you as you journal today.

JOHN 16:33

Verse:

"I have said these things to you, that in me you may have peace. In the world you will have tribulation. But take heart; I have overcome the world."

John 16:33

Context and prompt:

As we travel through the Advent season, we delight in the story of the story of the Nativity, imagining Mary and Elizabeth; Joseph and Gabriel; the shepherds; the star. It is easy to get swept up in the joyful expectation of the Nativity story. But when we focus not only on the birth of Christ, but also on the coming of Jesus into the world and into our lives, we develop another, deeper meaning to the Christmas story. Christmas is a time of peace not only because of the baby in a manger, but also because of the man that baby grew up to be.

This verse comes when Jesus is speaking with his disciples, and tells them that he is not alone, because God is with him. Jesus' disciples lived in a time of darkness, in which God's people often felt very far-removed from God and God's presence on earth. Jesus, in the incarnation, was the very opposite of that: God and person not far removed from each other, but one and the same in one person. In this verse, Jesus tells us to "have peace" and "take heart." We don't need to worry; he has overcome the world.

For today's verse, focus on the idea of overcoming. Maybe you'd like to journal about something you've overcome, whether that be a fear, an illness, or something else. You could also choose to journal the image of Jesus, overcoming the world in victory over death. Finally, you might choose to letter the words "take heart; I have overcome the world" in the margins of your Bible as you journal today.

—

2 THESSALONIANS 3:16

Verse:

"Now may the Lord of peace himself give you peace at all times in every way. The Lord be with you all."

2 Thessalonians 3:16

Context and prompt:

Today's verse is the benediction, or blessing given, at the end of the second letter to the Thessalonians. Though its words are simple, this blessing holds power. It reminds us that our God is a god of peace, and extends to us the hope that that God will bless us with that same peace. The blessing closes with the call for the Lord to be with us. Though God is always present, when we carry peace in our hearts and act with peace in the world, we are helping to spread grace and love to places where God's presence may otherwise not be felt. We are carrying God with us, and spreading God's peace to others.

For today's verse, focus on the ways in which we have studied peace throughout this week. We began with the imagery of the mountain, and then of strength. After experiencing the visitation to Mary and her Magnificat, we thought about peace in the context of victory. In a world as violent and troubled as our own, seeing peace as a steady, strong, and victorious quality may be unusual. But in the face of hardship, the attitude of peace, in which we "take heart" as Jesus said, truly is one of victory.

As you journal today, focus on the imagery of peace. The image of the dove has often been a symbol of peace, as has the rainbow. You might want to illustrate these symbols on your page; a dove holding an olive branch like in the Noah story, or a rainbow covering the sky. You could also choose to letter a phrase from the text that was meaningful to you, such as "peace at all times in every way." However you choose to journal this last entry in our week of peace, allow the lessons and verses from this week to guide you.

—

THIRD WEEK OF ADVENT

Welcome to the third week of Advent! We are now halfway through our Advent journey together; I hope that this time has already been helping you prepare your heart and mind for Christmas Day.

Today is Sunday, a time of rest for everyone journaling with us this Advent. If you are looking forward to journaling or took rest days throughout last week, today would be a great time to catch up on missed entries or to prepare for this coming week of journaling. But for those of us who are looking for a little peace in a hectic Advent season - as I think many of us are - I want to encourage you to take this day to fully, truly rest.

Last week, we journaled through the theme of Peace as we lit the second candle in our Advent wreath. We began by remembering that God can be a place of peace in times of store, and moved through the week noting peace as a source of strength and victory. This week, we are moving on to the third candle in our Advent wreath, the rose-colored candle of Love.

This week's candle is a different color from the others because it is a week of celebration and joy, rather than one of penitence. This week, we celebrate God's love in the world, both in the story of the Nativity and in our own lives and interactions with each other. As we journal this week, I encourage you to look for and create moments of love and grace in your life. Enjoy this moment of rest, and I look forward to journaling with you tomorrow!

—

LEVITICUS 19:18

Verse:

You shall not take vengeance or bear a grudge against the sons of your own people, but you shall love your neighbor as yourself: I am the Lord.

Leviticus 19:18

Context and prompt:

For each week of this Advent challenge, we begin the weekly study in a place of longing and reflection. In our first week of Advent, we reflected on the absence of light and the coming of hope through the expectation of a savior. In the second week, we reflected on the stability of God's peace in times of human violence, and moved towards resting in the peace that God has planned for us. Today, we begin with the vengeance and grudges which we are called to turn from. As the week progresses, we hope to move to a place of deep love, for God and for humanity.

In today's verse, God calls God's people to love their neighbors as themselves. Many of us have heard these words before, and may not have realized that they don't come from the mouth of Jesus, but from the book of Leviticus. This command to love one another is woven throughout both the Old and New Testaments, and is later not only repeated, but amplified by Jesus in the Gospels.

Today, we think about the concept of "neighbors," both next door and far away. What does it mean to love our neighbors as ourselves? How could showing love and charity to our neighbors be a reflection of God's love for them?

Today, think of the concept of neighbors as you journal. You might want to show two people helping each other tend to a shared garden, or you could show people holding hands around the world. You could also letter the words "Love your neighbor" over the page. There are no rules as you journal today; just let your love for God and God's creation guide you as you journal!

—

PSALM 59:16

Verse:

But I will sing of your strength;
I will sing aloud of your steadfast love in the morning.
For you have been to me a fortress
and a refuge in the day of my distress.

Psalm 59:16

Context and prompt:

Few books in the Bible resonate with so many people as the Psalms. Tradition holds that the Psalms were written by King David; that they tell of his distress and despair as well as his deep faith and love for God. In this verse, the writer of the psalm speaks of both trouble - the day of his distress - and celebration: singing of God's strength and steadfast love.

As you journal today, think of Bible journaling as your special way of singing out loud about God's love. What has God done in your life lately that is worth celebrating or singing about? Maybe you see God's love in your family, church, or community. Maybe you see it reflected in the actions of a person you admire. Or maybe you are in a position where God's love is not always visible, and you have the ability to be an example of grace and mercy. Whatever your situation, let this journaling entry be a celebration of God's steadfast love, drawing a heart, a scene that exemplifies love to you, or lettering the words "your steadfast love." Let the spirit of celebration and gratitude guide you as you journal today!

MATTHEW 1:18-25

Verse:

Now the birth of Jesus Christ took place in this way. When his mother Mary had been betrothed to Joseph, before they came together she was found to be with child from the Holy Spirit. And her husband Joseph, being a just man and unwilling to put her to shame, resolved to divorce her quietly. But as he considered these things, behold, an angel of the Lord appeared to him in a dream, saying, "Joseph, son of David, do not fear to take Mary as your wife, for that which is conceived in her is from the Holy Spirit. She will bear a son, and you shall call his name Jesus, for he will save his people from their sins." All this took place to fulfill what the Lord had spoken by the prophet:
"Behold, the virgin shall conceive and bear a son,
and they shall call his name Immanuel"
(which means, God with us). When Joseph woke from sleep, he did as the angel of the Lord commanded him: he took his wife, but knew her not until she had given birth to a son. And he called his name Jesus.

Matthew 1:18-25

Context and prompt:

In last week's Story reading, we experienced the visitation of the angel Gabriel to Mary, and her wonder and joy at being pregnant. Today, we hear Joseph's side of the story. After finding out that his intended wife was pregnant, Joseph intended to quietly divorce her, rather than making a public spectacle or putting her to shame. But the Holy Spirit came to Joseph and told him about God's plan for Mary and for her child, relating the pregnancy back to a prophecy from the book of Isaiah. Joseph woke from the dream and did as the angel had told him, staying with Mary through her pregnancy and the birth of Jesus, and remaining her husband after that.

Just as last week we focused on Mary, for today's verse and journaling entry, we focus on Joseph and his visit from the Holy Spirit. You might choose to illustrate Joseph sleeping and being visited by the angel Gabriel. You could also choose to illustrate the message of Gabriel's words to Joseph, showing the baby Jesus lying in a manger. Finally, you might choose to letter a phrase from the passage, such as the name "Immanuel," which translates to God with us. Whichever direction you choose to take this verse in, allow your excitement for the coming of Christmas to guide you as you journal today!

SONG
—
LUKE 1:68-79 –
BENEDICTUS

Verse:

"Blessed be the Lord God of Israel,
for he has visited and redeemed his people
and has raised up a horn of salvation for us
in the house of his servant David,
as he spoke by the mouth of his holy prophets from of old,
that we should be saved from our enemies
and from the hand of all who hate us;
to show the mercy promised to our fathers
and to remember his holy covenant,
the oath that he swore to our father Abraham, to grant us
that we, being delivered from the hand of our enemies,
might serve him without fear,
in holiness and righteousness before him all our days.
And you, child, will be called the prophet of the Most High;
for you will go before the Lord to prepare his ways,
to give knowledge of salvation to his people
in the forgiveness of their sins,
because of the tender mercy of our God,
whereby the sunrise shall visit us from on high
to give light to those who sit in darkness and in the shadow of death,
to guide our feet into the way of peace."

Luke 1:68-79

Context and prompt:

The Benedictus, also called the "Song of Zechariah," is the song that Zechariah sings at the oath of circumcision and naming of his son, John. As you may remember from last week's Song day, Zechariah is the husband of Elizabeth and the father to John the Baptist. After the angel Gabriel visits him and tells him that he and Elizabeth will have a son, Zechariah doubts him because he and Elizabeth are already advanced in age. Gabriel announces that Zechariah will not be able to speak until the events in his words come to pass. Only eight days after the birth of his son, when Zechariah writes on a tablet that his name is John (rather than a family name), does Zechariah regain his ability to speak. Not only that, but he can sing - and he sings the verses above, the Benedictus, which comes from the Latin opening to the canticle, meaning "Blessed be."

Especially beautiful in Zechariah's song are the lines he sings directly to his newborn son: "And you, child, will be called the prophet of the Most High; for you will go before the Lord to prepare his ways, to give knowledge of salvation to his people in the forgiveness of their sins, because of the tender mercy of our God" (Luke 1:76-78). These are the verses that we'll be focusing on on our journaling efforts today.

In the margins or pages of your Bible, focus on the figure of John the Baptist, who in his adult years made way for God and let them know of "the tender mercy of God." You might choose to illustrate John as he proclaims and makes way for Jesus. Or you could choose to illustrate him as he baptizes Jesus, as happens in Matthew 3. Or, if you're moved by the image of Zechariah singing to his newborn son, you might choose to illustrate him singing to the infant John, lettering the words "And you, child." Let the spirit of love move you as you journal in your Bible today!

–

JOHN 13:34-35

Verse:

"A new commandment I give to you, that you love one another: just as I have loved you, you also are to love one another. By this all people will know that you are my disciples, if you have love for one another."

John 13:34-35

Context and prompt:

One of the things that most often draws people to the Christian faith is the love and mercy of Jesus. Today's selection is a beautiful example of not only the kind of love that is given to us, but also the love that we are called to give to each other. This verse comes in the Gospel of John, when Jesus is speaking to his disciples. This is the first of two times in the Fourth Gospel that Jesus issues the command to love one another, and although the Israelites were told to love their neighbors as they loved themselves in Leviticus 19:18, this command is much weightier. The way to love each other is no longer as we love ourselves, but instead to love each other as Jesus loves us.

As we move towards Christmas Day, reflect on Jesus' legacy of love, not just in his disciples, but in us. Focus on the image of the disciples who loved and followed Jesus. Just as they sat at the feet of Jesus and tried to love each other as he said to, we also learn how to live and love from his example. Let these disciples inspire you as you journal today. You might want to journal the disciples sitting at the feet of Jesus, listening, or washing each others' feet in an act of humble love. You could also think of modern followers of Jesus, showing love to each other and to mankind through acts of service or charity. Finally, if you have trouble thinking of an image you'd like to journal today, you could letter the words "love one another" over an image of the world or a flurry of hearts. Don't worry about getting it 'wrong' or 'right.' Focus on how this verse speaks to you and how you want to put that on the page as you journal today.

—

1 CORINTHIANS 13:4-8

Verse:

Love is patient and kind; love does not envy or boast; it is not arrogant or rude. It does not insist on its own way; it is not irritable or resentful; it does not rejoice at wrongdoing, but rejoices with the truth. Love bears all things, believes all things, hopes all things, endures all things.
Love never ends. As for prophecies, they will pass away; as for tongues, they will cease; as for knowledge, it will pass away.

1 Corinthians 13:4-8

Context and prompt:

This verse from Paul's letter to the Corinthians is often read at weddings and other events, and with reason! Paul's words on the nature of a true and lasting love inspire us to love each other better. Throughout this week, we have journaled the theme of love and traced it through the Bible: first in the command to love our neighbors as ourselves in Leviticus, then in the Psalmist's loving songs to God, through Joseph's love for Mary, Zechariah's love for his son John, and the disciples' love for one another. Today, as we get nearer to Christmas Day and the coming of the baby Jesus, we are celebrating the love woven throughout the Bible.

In today's journal entry, do your best to celebrate the love that we have studied and experienced in our study this week. You could choose to do a big creative celebration of love, pulling in many colors, patterns, or tools to show the feeling of love. Or you could journal about those you love, using photos or sketches of your family or other loved ones. Do your best to have fun with this verse and be creative as you journal the last entry in our Love week!

—

FOURTH WEEK OF ADVENT

Welcome to the fourth and final week of Advent! During the last three weeks, we have journaled through the weekly themes of Hope, Peace, and Love. I hope and pray that these weeks have been meaningful and helpful for you in appreciating Advent and preparing yourself for Christmas Day!

Today is a rest day for everyone in our Bible journaling community, whether they are journaling just once weekly, or six days per week. If you rested throughout last week, or are eager to prepare for journaling this coming week, then now would be a great time to catch up on previous entries or to prepare your pages for the coming few days. If, however, you need a little rest (as most of us do), then please use this time as a sabbath from your journaling practice.

Today we begin the final week of Advent, lighting the candle of Joy in our Advent wreath and journaling through the joy of the birth of Jesus. This is the last week before Christmas, so our Nativity story reaches its crescendo as we experience the birth of Christ and the celebration of the world. Though this week will adopt the same schedule and rhythm of the other weeks, beginning with an Old Testament verse and a Psalm and moving through the Gospels to the closing letters of the Bible, there will be a common thread of joy and celebration throughout this week. I hope that joy inspires you to celebrate the Nativity and, this time next week, Christmas Day!

—

NEHEMIAH 8:10

Verse:

Then he said to them, "Go your way. Eat the fat and drink sweet wine and send portions to anyone who has nothing ready, for this day is holy to our Lord. And do not be grieved, for the joy of the Lord is your strength."

Nehemiah 8:10

Context and prompt:

Every week, we begin our study of a topic by noting its absence. In our first week, we moved from hopelessness to hope; in the second, from violence to peace; and in the third, from resentment to love. Today is no different. Though we will not be journaling about the absence of joy, this verse about joy comes from a time that was very challenging for the people of God. In the Babylonian exile, the Israelites were forced to leave their home city of Jerusalem, and were only permitted to return several generations later. In their time away, many of them had forgotten or abandoned the beliefs of their ancestors. When, in the books of Ezra and Nehemiah, they are reminded of these rites and practices, they turn to weeping and anguish. Nehemiah, one of their leaders, acknowledges the importance of mourning, but also tells them to enjoy their lives and remember that "the joy of the Lord is [their] strength."

Finding and feeling the joy of the Lord is one of the most rewarding aspects of a spiritual life. Often we forget, as the Israelites did, that we can return to this joy no matter how long we've been away. Today, give yourself a few minutes to center yourself and focus your mind on the parts of your faith life that are most rewarding for you. As you think about the things that make you feel the "joy of the Lord," begin putting those things to paper. What connects you to God? If it is Bible studies or devotionals, you might want to letter or illustrate a line from a recent study that has really stuck with you. If you find yourself most invigorated and 'lit up' from within during church or group worship, perhaps you could journal your church or the faces of people in your community. Or maybe you feel most at one with God when wandering through God's creation, experiencing the sunset or watching ducks swim on the lake. In that case, journal a nature scene that inspires you. If none of these ideas work for you, try lettering the phrase "the joy of the Lord" in a way that is meaningful to you! May joy encompass you as you journal today.

—

PSALM 30:5

Verse:

For his anger is but for a moment,
and his favor is for a lifetime.
Weeping may tarry for the night,
but joy comes with the morning.

Psalm 30:5

Context and prompt:

"Joy comes in the morning." These words could maybe not be more true than now, so close to Christmas! Imagine the delight of a child on Christmas morning, opening gifts and spending time with the people who love and cherish her. Any nightmares or remnants of yesterday are gone. All she experiences right now is pure joy.

Often, when we struggle to make our way through times that challenge and even defeat us, we find comfort in the idea that tomorrow is a new day. Maybe next week will be better. Maybe, come next year, things will be different. That is one of the messages that this verse gives to us; though we may be subject to anger or weep for a night, God's favor is lasting, and joy comes in the morning. Sometimes, that joy is bittersweet, and sometimes it is an all-encompassing, un-self-conscious joy that takes over our whole beings like it does for a child on Christmas Day.

We are only a few days away from Christmas, and tomorrow we will be journaling the story of the Nativity. As you wait for the joy of tomorrow and of Christmas morning, reflect on and journal the idea of morning. Maybe you'd like to paint a sunrise, or the dew on the grass at dawn. You could also choose to journal the joy of children on Christmas morning, or journal a memory from your own family. Finally, you could choose to letter the words "joy comes in the morning." Let the joy and excitement of Christmas sweep you up as you journal today!

LUKE 2:1, 2:4-14

Verse:

In those days a decree went out from Caesar Augustus that all the world should be registered… And Joseph also went up from Galilee, from the town of Nazareth, to Judea, to the city of David, which is called Bethlehem, because he was of the house and lineage of David, to be registered with Mary, his betrothed, who was with child. And while they were there, the time came for her to give birth. And she gave birth to her firstborn son and wrapped him in swaddling cloths and laid him in a manger, because there was no place for them in the inn. And in the same region there were shepherds out in the field, keeping watch over their flock by night. And an angel of the Lord appeared to them, and the glory of the Lord shone around them, and they were filled with great fear. And the angel said to them, "Fear not, for behold, I bring you good news of great joy that will be for all the people. For unto you is born this day in the city of David a Savior, who is Christ the Lord. And this will be a sign for you: you will find a baby wrapped in swaddling cloths and lying in a manger." And suddenly there was with the angel a multitude of the heavenly host praising God and saying,
"Glory to God in the highest,
and on earth peace among those with whom he is pleased!"

Luke 2:11-12

Context and prompt:

After three weeks of journey through the themes of

the Advent wreath, and exploring the stages of the Nativity story, we finally arrive at the birth of Jesus. As we learn from these verses and remember from years of Christmas pageants, Jesus was born under unusual circumstances. After the emperor ordered that all his subjects had to register themselves in a census, Joseph and a heavily pregnant Mary had to travel back to his hometown of Bethlehem. Because there was no room for them in the nearby inn, Mary gave birth and laid her son in a manger, the long box from which the animals would eat. While this has led many people to believe that she also gave birth in a barn, the text itself does not tell us. What we do know is that the Son of God was not only given to an unwed mother to bear, but born in humble circumstances. What a beautiful reminder that God's love and mercy extends to those in even the most humble places.

Today's verse also includes the visit of the angel to the shepherds in the field. After the angel of the Lord tells the shepherds the "good news of great joy" of the birth of Jesus, a chorus of angels appear and sing, joyfully, of Glory to God and peace on earth.

Today's verse is a beautiful and meaningful one, because it not only tells us of the birth of Jesus, but also of the celebration and joy that followed. Journal, today, how you imagine the Nativity scene. Maybe it's a traditional scene with Mary, Joseph, and the baby Jesus in the barn. Maybe the barn is in the distance as you illustrate the shepherds hearing the music of the angels. Or maybe you prefer to letter the words from this verse, writing out "good news of great joy" in a way that is meaningful for you. Though our community has not yet reached Christmas Day, today is really the first day in which we celebrate the birth and coming of Jesus Christ. Let that joy guide you in your journaling!

LUKE 2:29-32 – NUNC DIMITTIS

Verse:

"Lord, now you are letting your servant depart in peace,
according to your word;
for my eyes have seen your salvation
that you have prepared in the presence of all peoples,
a light for revelation to the Gentiles,
and for glory to your people Israel."

Luke 2:29-32

Context and prompt:

Nunc dimittis, also known as the Song of Simeon, is the third and final canticle or inner-Biblical hymn in the book of Luke. The story goes that Simeon was a devout man who had been promised that he would not die until he saw the Messiah. When Joseph and Mary took the baby Jesus to the temple for the ceremony of the consecration of the firstborn son, more than 40 days after Jesus' birth, Simeon saw the baby Jesus. He held Jesus in his arms and cried out the lines from today's reading, celebrating the coming of the Messiah and the salvation and light that this baby's coming signaled.

Today, as we are just a few days from the beauty and delight of Christmas Day, we journal about sight. Simeon was overjoyed to see Jesus with his own eyes, but we, too, have the ability to see light in our lives: not just visually, but also on a spiritual and emotional level. The light and love of God makes its way known especially in the life and legacy of Jesus, but also in the little moments and things all around us.

As you journal today, you could choose to journal an image of Simeon holding the baby Jesus, singing joyfully. You could also choose to make this verse more personal, journaling a moment where you felt that you saw the light of God in your own life. Finally, if you struggle to think of a visual way to illustrate this passage, consider lettering the words "My eyes have seen your salvation." Don't worry about getting the passage wrong or right; focus on journaling from the heart and using your joy to guide you as you journal today.

—

MATTHEW 2:9-11

Verse:

*After listening to the king, they went on their way. And
behold, the star that they had seen when it rose went before them until
it came to rest over the place where the child was. When they saw the
star, they rejoiced exceedingly with great joy. And going into the house,
they saw the child with Mary his mother, and they fell down and
worshiped him. Then, opening their treasures, they offered him gifts,
gold and frankincense and myrrh.*

Matthew 2:9-11

Context and prompt:

In today's reading, King Herod sends three wise
men to find the baby people are worshipping in Bethlehem.
These wise men are guided by a star to the house where
Mary and the baby Jesus are, and they fall down to their
knees to worship him, giving him the famous 'gifts of the
magi,' or wise men: gold, frankincense, and myrrh. Imagine
the wonder and delight of these wise men, who see that the
prophecies they have studied their entire lives have been
fulfilled. Imagine their joy! We hope to share in this joy this
season and every Christmas: that hope, peace, and love
have come to earth and are ours to inherit.

As you journal this verse today, focus on the image
of the three wise men, also called the magi. You might want
to illustrate the wise men themselves, perhaps as kings

from different parts of the world, as they are often represented in art and films. You could also choose to focus on the gifts being given to the baby Jesus, imagining the splendor of these beautiful offerings, which some say are themselves symbols for the fulfillment of prophecy. Finally, you could choose to letter a few words from the passage, such as "rejoice exceedingly with great joy." This is a time of celebration, of adoration, and of worship. Do your best to express what you feel about this Christmas season as you journal in your Bible today!

SCRIPTURE – EPISTLE
–
1 PETER 1:8-9

Verse:

Though you have not seen him, you love him. Though you do not now see him, you believe in him and rejoice with joy that is inexpressible and filled with glory, obtaining the outcome of your faith, the salvation of your souls.

1 Peter 1:8-9

Context and prompt:

It's here! After four weeks of journaling through the themes of Hope, Peace, Love, and Joy, we have finally made our way to Christmas. As we found hope in the coming of this season, peace in trusting God, love for our fellow people, and joy at the impending celebration of Christmas, we prepared our hearts and minds for this day: Christmas, the day when we celebrate the birth of Christ.

The verse above, taken from Paul's letter to the Corinthians, celebrates the inexpressible joy we hope to all someday find in our journeys with God. Through Advent, we wait for the coming of the Christ child, reflecting on the things that are not-yet and the things that are to come. But now, on this last day of Advent, we experience a joyful and celebration at the things that are. As we celebrate the birth of Jesus, we remember to also look at the legacy that his life and lessons left for us; the bonds that have been broken; the hearts that have been poured full with love and mercy and grace. All these things given to us from the life that began in an infant, lying in a manger, in the little town of Bethlehem.

As you journal today's entry, focus on the feelings of joy and celebration that you feel at the coming of Christmas. You can focus on one of the images or themes from this study that spoke to you, tying in expectation, fulfillment, or tradition. Or you can journal an image of the baby Jesus on this last day of Advent, before we celebrate his birth tomorrow, on Christmas Day.

CLOSING WORDS FOR CHRISTMAS DAY

Merry Christmas! After four weeks of journaling through scripture and focusing on the themes of the Advent wreath, our community has now made our way through Advent and to the beautiful celebration of Christmas Day. I hope that these weeks of preparation have allowed you to center yourself during a busy holiday season, and given you the tools to prepare your heart for the meaning and value of Christmas and all that it represents.

Advent is among my favorite seasons because it centers around that which is not-yet. But the season of Christmas is one of fulfillment: it is an exciting, comforting, and joyful season of what has already been done, and the ways that God has already fulfilled God's promises to us. So during this season of Christmas, as you experience not only Christmas Day but the eleven Christmas days thereafter, focus on and celebrate what is already, and on the things that God has given and fulfilled in your life. Whether given to the mind, body, or soul, these are the true gifts of Christmas.

I hope that the coming season is one of hope, peace, love, and joy for you as this Advent has been; but also one of fulfillment, of celebration, and of gifts. Thank you for joining us for Advent Illustrated this season, and once again, Merry Christmas!

ABOUT THE AUTHOR

Sara Laughed is a writer, blogger, and student of Religion. After beginning Bible journaling just before her confirmation, she began writing journaling studies in the fall of 2015 with *Advent Illustrated: Journey Through the Bible*, which saw 2,000 participants creatively journaling through the Advent season together. Since then, Seasons Illustrated studies have been read and journaled all over the world.

Sara most enjoys learning and spending time with loved ones. She is immensely grateful for the opportunity to share in Advent with you this year and wishes you a joyful and meaningful holiday season.

RESOURCES AND LINKS

This study includes access to a variety of extra resources and downloads.

We have a series of weekly videos for the study, available at our YouTube channel Seasons Illustrated, which you can access at http://bit.ly/advent-videos

There are free downloads, including a printable Advent calendar and a daily verse bookmark, on our site Seasons Illustrated. You can access the Advent Library at http://seasonsillustrated.com/advent-library using the password: **joy**

Our Facebook group is a great community to keep you inspired. Join us by searching for "Seasons Illustrated" on Facebook or by going to https://www.facebook.com/groups/seasonsillustrated/

You can also follow us on social media for updates:

Facebook: **/seasonsillustrated**
Instagram: **@seasonsillustrated**
Twitter: **@seasillustrated**
Pinterest: **@seasillustrated**

#adventillustrated
#seasonsillustrated

57670162R00053

Made in the USA
Lexington, KY
21 November 2016